CHANEY-MONGE SCHOOL DIST. #88
400 ELSIE AVENUE
CREST HILL, IL 60403

636.5
Hus

Chicken

$20

(HC)

CHANEY-MONGE SCHOOL DIST. #88
400 ELSIE AVENUE
CREST HILL, IL 60403

2008/09

DEMCO

26

Looking at Life Cycles

Chicken

Victoria Huseby

A⁺

Smart Apple Media

Smart Apple Media is published by Black Rabbit Books
P.O. Box 3263, Mankato, Minnesota 56002

Printed in the United States

Published by arrangement with the Watts Publishing Group Ltd, London.

Editor: Rachel Tonkin
Designer: Chris Fraser
Illustrator: John Alston
Picture researcher: Diana Morris
Science consultant: Andrew Solway
Literacy consultant: Gill Matthews

Picture credits:
DK Images: 17; Robert Dowling/Corbis: front cover, 1;
William Gottlieb/Corbis: 21; Julie Habel/Corbis: 5, 15;
Wayne Hutchinson/Photographers Direct: 19;
Peter Kubal/Photographers Direct: 9;
Robert Pickett/Ecoscene: 7, 11, 13.

Library of Congress Cataloging-in-Publication Data

Huseby, Victoria.
    Chicken / by Victoria Huseby.
    p. cm.— (Smart Apple Media. Looking at life cycles)
    Summary: "An introduction to the life cycle of a chicken from egg to adult"—
Provided by publisher.
    Includes index.
    ISBN 978-1-59920-175-7
    1. Chickens—Life cycles—Juvenile literature. I. Title.
SF487.5.H87 2009
636.5—dc22

                                                                    2007030459

9 8 7 6 5 4 3 2 1

Contents

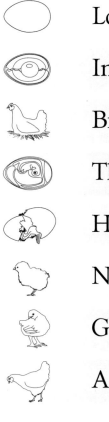

Laying an Egg

A female chicken is called a hen. She makes a **nest** with straw. She lays her **eggs** in the nest. Each egg has a new chick inside it.

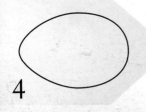

Inside an Egg

At first, the chicken inside the egg is just a tiny dot. It is called an **embryo**. The yellow **yolk** in the egg has food in it. The food helps the embryo grow.

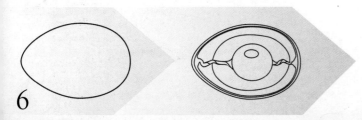

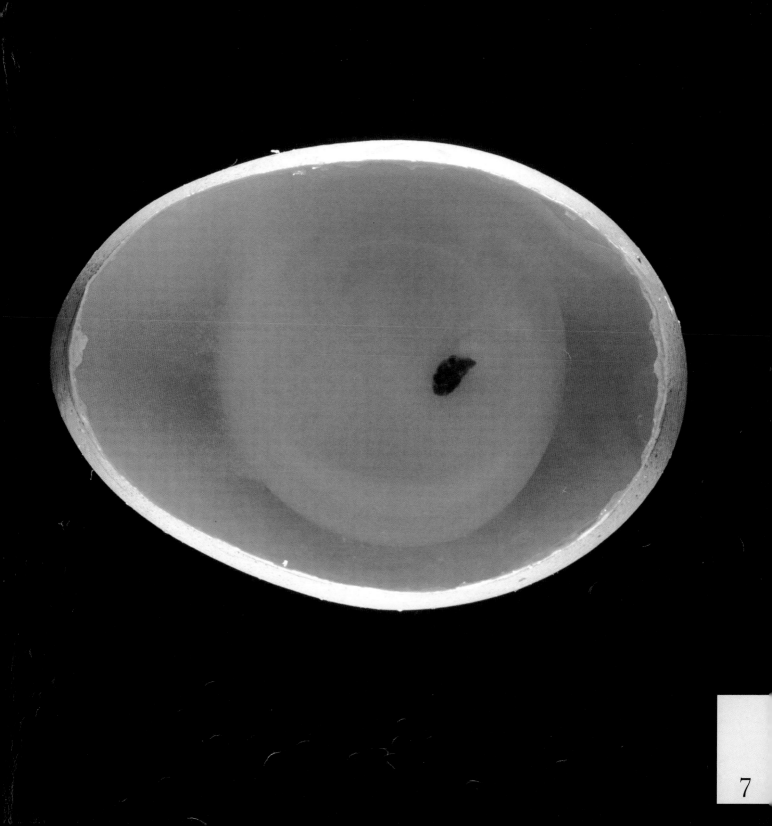

7

Brooding

The hen helps the embryos grow by sitting on the eggs. She keeps them warm and safe. This is called **brooding**.

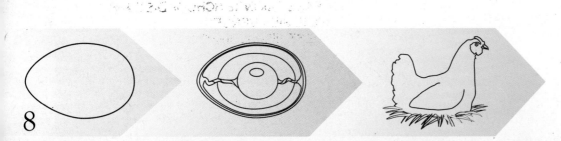

9

The Embryo Grows

As the embryo grows, it is protected by a soft, jellylike substance called **albumen**. Like the yolk, it has food in it.

11

Hatching

After three weeks, the chick
is ready to hatch. It uses
a special tooth on its beak
called an **egg tooth** to
break out of the egg. The
chick is wet when it hatches.

New Chick

The chick soon dries out.
It has fluffy yellow feathers,
called **down**. The chick can
walk as soon as it hatches.

Growing Up

As the chick gets older,
it grows new feathers.
It starts to look like an
adult chicken.

CHANEY-MONGE SCHOOL DIST. #88
400 ELSIE AVENUE
CREST HILL, IL 60403

Adulthood

In a few months, the chick
is fully grown. Chickens peck
the ground looking for food.
They eat grain and worms.

Making a Nest

When a female chicken
is about five months old,
she is ready to build a nest. She
will lay eggs and have chicks
of her own.

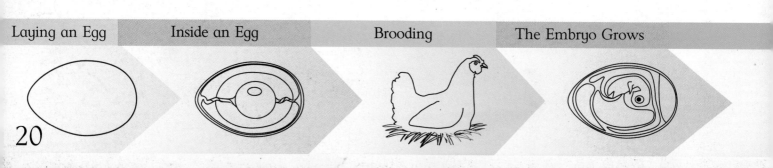

Hatching   New Chick   Growing Up   Adulthood

Chicken Facts

- There are many different types of chickens. They can be different sizes and colors.

- Only eggs that have been fertilized by a rooster will hatch into chicks. The eggs we eat do not have a chick inside them.

- A male chicken is called a rooster.

- It takes a chicken about 24 hours to make one egg.

- Chickens have wings, but they cannot fly far.

- Chickens eat insects, worms, slugs, grain, and other things they find on the ground.

- Chickens can lay between 250 and 300 eggs every year.

- Chickens can live for as long as seven years.

Glossary

Albumen
The white part of the egg that protects the embryo as it is growing.

Brooding
When a hen keeps her eggs warm by sitting on them.

Down
Soft, fluffy feathers that cover a young chick.

Egg
Contains the baby chicken, surrounded by yolk and albumen.

Egg tooth
A tiny tooth-like point on the tip of a chick's beak. The chick uses the egg tooth to break out of the egg.

Embryo
The early stage of a young animal when it is growing inside an egg or inside its mother.

Nest
A hollow place built or used by a bird as a home to rear its young.

Yolk
The yellow part of the egg that has food for the embryo.

Index and Web Sites

For Kids:

Farm Animals
http://www.kidsfarm.com

Life Cycle of a Chicken
http://www.vtaide.com/png/chicken.htm

For Teachers:

A to Z Teacher Stuff: Life Cycles
http://atozteacherstuff.com/Themes/
    Life_Cycles/

Pro Teacher! Life Science Lesson Plans
http://www.proteacher.com/110003.shtml

HOME PLATE HEIST

STONE ARCH BOOKS

a capstone imprint

JAKE MADDOX
GRAPHIC NOVELS

Published by Stone Arch Books,
an imprint of Capstone.
1710 Roe Crest Drive
North Mankato, Minnesota 56003
www.capstonepub.com

Library of Congress Cataloging-in-Publication Data Names:
Mauleón, Daniel, 1991– author. | Vitrano, Erika, artist. |
   Reed, Jaymes, letterer. | Muñiz, Berenice, cover artist.
Title: Home plate heist / text by Daniel Mauleón ; art by
   Erika Vitrano ; lettering by Jaymes Reed ; cover art by
   Berenice Muñiz.
Description: North Mankato, Minnesota : Stone Arch Books,
   [2021] | Series: Jake Maddox graphic novels | Includes
   bibliographical references. | Audience: Ages 8–11. |
   Audience: Grades 4–6.
Identifiers: LCCN 2020025553 (print) | LCCN 2020025554
   (ebook) | ISBN 9781515882312 (library binding) | ISBN
   9781515883401 (paperback) | ISBN 9781515892021 (ebook pdf)
Subjects: CYAC: Baseball—Fiction. | Self-confidence—Fiction. |
   Family life—Fiction. | Hispanic Americans—Fiction.
Classification: LCC PZ7.7.M3884 Hom 2021 (print) | LCC
   PZ7.7.M3884 (ebook) | DDC 741.5/973—dc23
LC record available at https://lccn.loc.gov/2020025553
LC ebook record available at https://lccn.loc.gov/2020025554

Summary: Fernando Higuera loves playing baseball.
The game is in his blood. He comes from a family of skilled
baseball players. However, during one game Fernando's coach
tells him to try a new move and steal second base. But he's
never tried that before. Fernando hesitates and ends up getting
tagged out. He feels he let his team and family down. Luckily,
his family has his back and teaches him everything they know
about stealing bases. Will their advice help Fernando lead his
team to victory at the next big game?

Editor: Aaron Sautter
Designer: Brann Garvey
Production Specialist: Tori Abraham

Printed and bound in the USA. PO 3837

HOME PLATE HEIST

Text by Daniel Mauleón

Art by Erika Vitrano

Color by Francesca Ingrassia
and Giulia Campobello
(Grafimated Cartoon)

Lettering by Jaymes Reed

LANG

YUSUF

ABUELO

6

... it's my speed. Ever since I was little, I could run. I've always been the fastest kid. I know I'm the fastest on my team, the Green Lightning Bugs.

Abuelo says I'll be a great batter like him some day. But batting isn't my specialty . . .

I'm probably the fastest in the summer league. For me, a line drive is an easy base.

POP!

When Yusuf is up to bat, he gets a fantastic hit. But I don't stop to stare.

CRACK!

Instead I bolt off of first base. In a flash I touch second, but I know I can keep going.

I can always trust Yusuf to get a clean hit. And he knows I can make a great play. I like being reliable and someone my teammates can trust.

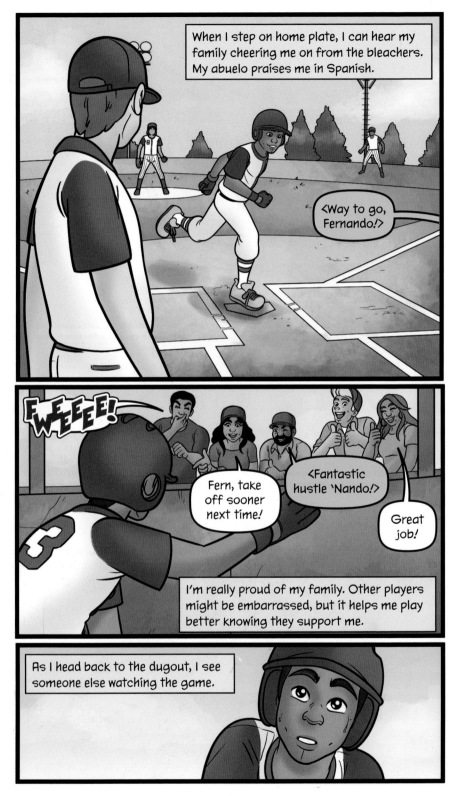

12

I don't recognize him. But for some reason he gives me a bad vibe . . .

His eyes suddenly lock on mine, and a chill goes down my spine.

14

15

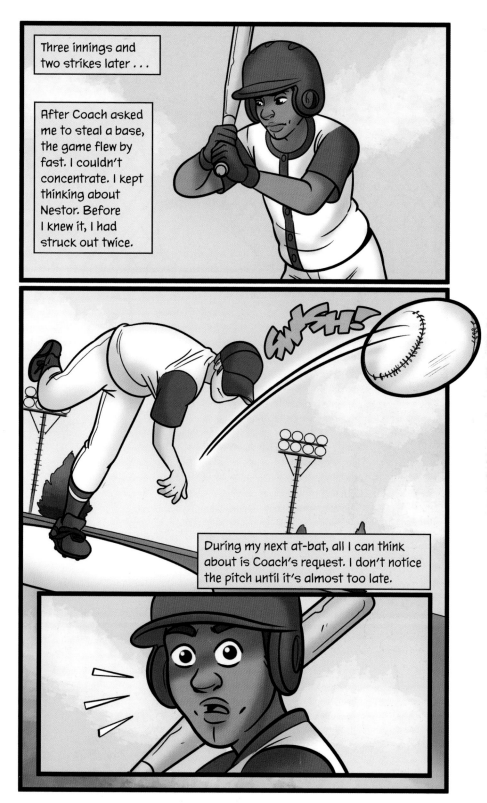

CRACK!

Thankfully, I get a hit. It's not great, but I take off running.

Safe!

It's good that I'm fast because I almost don't make it to first base.

Waiting over there is second base, just ninety feet away.

I can't explain it. Second base suddenly feels like it's a mile away. There's no way I can make it.

23

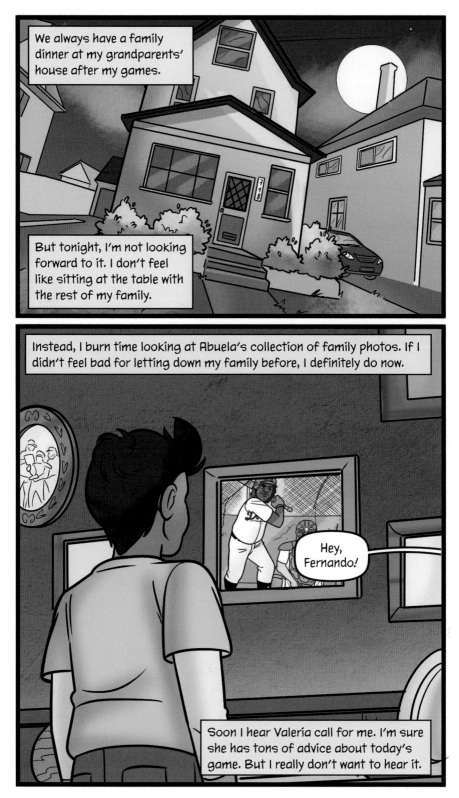

We always have a family dinner at my grandparents' house after my games.

But tonight, I'm not looking forward to it. I don't feel like sitting at the table with the rest of my family.

Instead, I burn time looking at Abuela's collection of family photos. If I didn't feel bad for letting down my family before, I definitely do now.

Hey, Fernando!

Soon I hear Valeria call for me. I'm sure she has tons of advice about today's game. But I really don't want to hear it.

26

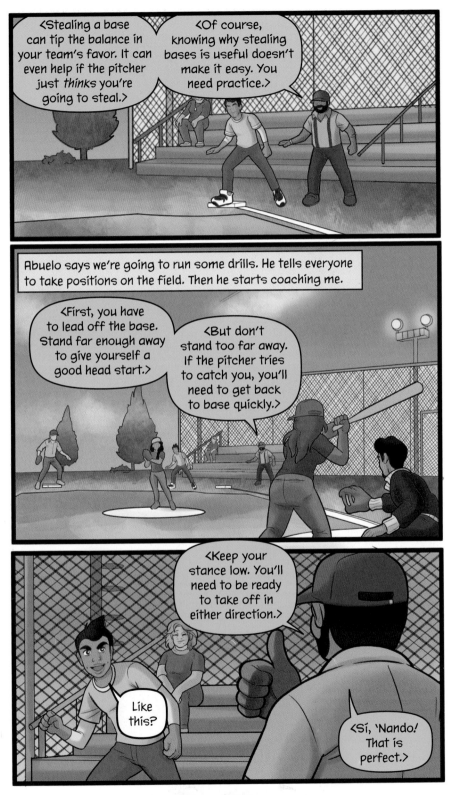

31

33

35

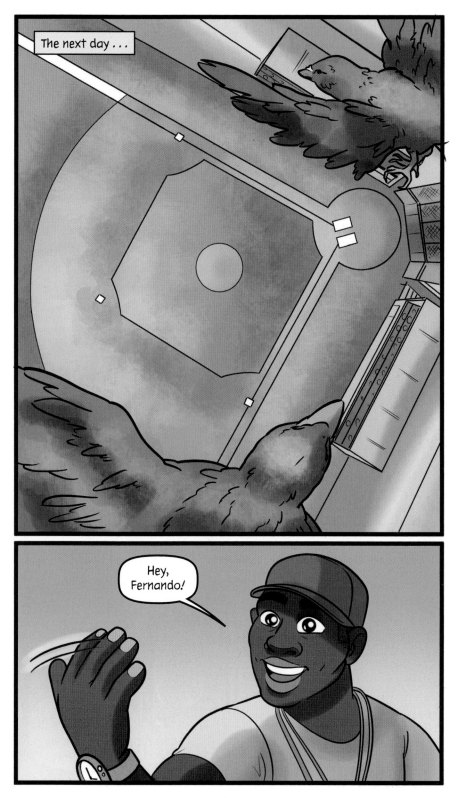

40

When I take my first at-bat I realize something important. I spent the whole week practicing how to steal second. But I didn't practice batting at all.

When Nestor launches a fastball at me, my mistake becomes very clear.

STRIKE ONE!

When Nestor's pitch zips past me, I barely even blink.

The second pitch drops through the strike zone with perfect accuracy.

STRIKE TWO!

STRIKE THREE! YOU'RE OUT!

THFP!

Nestor is no joke. I'm no longer worried about stealing second base. I'm worried about even getting to first.

<Hey! 'Nando!>

43

44

Over the next few innings, I watch Nestor closely. His pitches are slower than my sister's.

But his wind-up is much faster. He's focused. Accurate. Confident. My second and third at-bats go as well as my first. Nestor is the real deal.

At the bottom of the ninth inning the Yellow Jackets lead the game 2-0. Nestor is just one batter away from a shutout—me.

45

But I've watched Nestor for nine innings now. I can pick out the changes in his windup. This time, I'm ready.

47

Second base feels like it's a mile away. I told Coach I wasn't going to steal. But to win this game, I need to put pressure on Nestor. I need to try.

But as I think about it, my mind starts racing. If I mess up, my team loses. But if I don't try, it could still be game over.

I think about the week of practice with my family. I can hear Abuelo's words in my mind.

<Lead off about ten feet. Get enough to gain an edge, but not too far that you can't dive back.>

<Keep your stance wide. Be ready to explode in either direction.>

<Watch the pitcher and wait for the right moment.>

I do as I was trained. Right now, Nestor is confident and doesn't pay any attention to me. I wait for the first signs of his wind-up. Then . . .

50

From the corner of my eye I see the baseball heading my way.

I leap and stretch out my arms to beat Nestor's throw. I'm not sure if it'll be enough, but I'm fully committed.

53

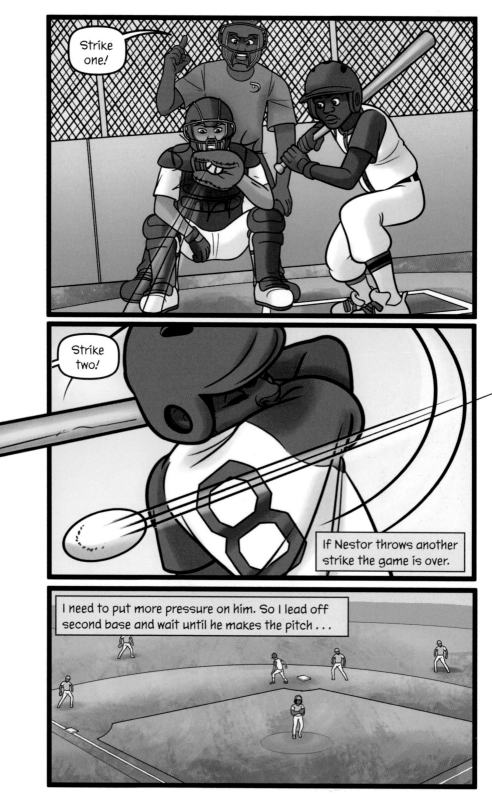

. . . then drive my body toward third base.

BALL!

I'm not sure if I'm lucky, or if Nestor saw me moving. But he throws a wild pitch. I get to third base, and Yusuf gets a full count.

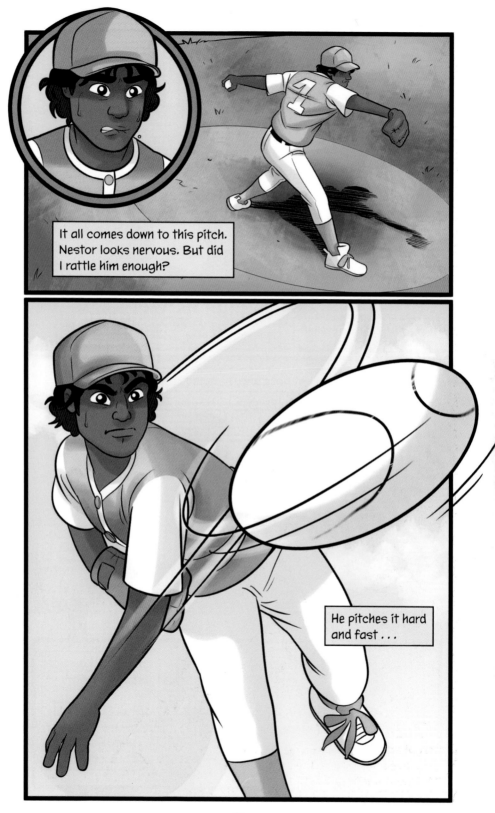

It all comes down to this pitch. Nestor looks nervous. But did I rattle him enough?

He pitches it hard and fast . . .

BALL FOUR!

I breathe a sigh of relief.

Yusuf gets a walk to first base and the count resets.

AT BAT	BALL	STRIKE	OUT	FIELD
11	0	0	2	

INNINGS

	1	2	3	4	5	6	7	8	9	10	RUNS	HITS	ERR
YELLOW STAG BEETLES	0	0	0	0	1	0	1	0	0		2	6	0
GREEN LIGHTNING BUGS	0	0	0	0	0	0	0	0			0	1	1

I make eye contact with Nestor. For the first time, I don't feel the chill down my spine. He no longer scares me. In fact . . .

59

When Lang is up to bat, he just needs one good pitch to bring me home. Maybe he can even get a triple so Yusuf can score and tie the game.

Lang smashes the ball and sends it flying!
I don't even need to sprint to home plate. I jog
home easily instead. Yusuf and I tie up the
score, and Lang brings home the winning run.

64

This week I learned that there's more to baseball than just hitting and running fast. You have to keep your head in the game. It's about outwitting your opponents as much as blasting home runs or pitching shutouts.

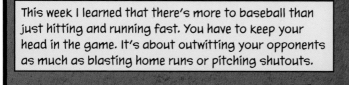

I'm thankful my family showed me that I could be a special player. And now I know I have a place in my abuelo's legacy.

THE END

1. Wide shots are used to tell the reader where a story takes place. What does the image to the left tell you about where Fernando's story happens?

2. Fernando is part of a very close family. How does the art in this panel show how they feel about him?

3. Closeups are often used to show what a character is thinking or feeling. What do you think Nestor is thinking about in this panel?

4. Graphic artists sometimes use extreme angles to add more drama to the story. How does the art show Fernando's feelings in this panel?

5. Graphic panels can be created in many ways. How do the panel shapes below help show what is happening in the story?

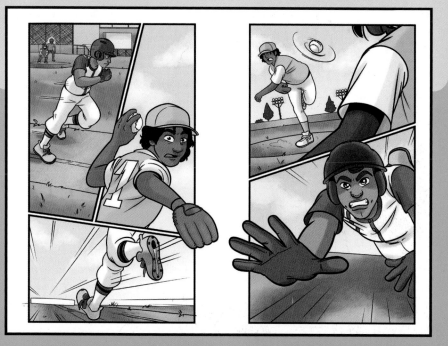

MORE ABOUT STEALING BASES

- Stealing bases has a long history in baseball. Skilled base stealers can help change the outcome of a game. In Major League Baseball runners must travel 90 feet (27.4 meters) between bases. The best players can do this in under three seconds.

- Rickey Henderson currently holds the career record for most stolen bases at 1,406. But stealing bases comes with some risk. Not surprisingly, Henderson also holds the record for the most times caught stealing at 335.

- Scientist and baseball fan David A. Peters discovered that sliding headfirst is faster than sliding feet first. This is partly because runners can extend their arms farther than their legs. They can also get a little boost of speed by pushing off the ground with their feet as they dive for the base.

MORE ABOUT PITCHING

- The best pitchers are known for more than just a powerful fastball. They use a variety of sneaky pitches to win games. Some of these include curve balls, screwballs, sliders, and more.

- Earned Run Average, or ERA, is an important statistic when talking about pitchers. ERA is the average number of runs scored against a pitcher if he or she plays a full game. The lower the ERA number, the more skilled the pitcher is.

- Cuban-American pitcher Aroldis Chapman threw the fastest pitch ever recorded. It screamed in at a whopping 105.1 miles (169.1 kilometers) per hour! Chapman threw the pitch while playing for the Cincinnati Reds in 2010. Five years later, Chapman tied his previous record while playing for the New York Yankees.

BASEBALL TERMS TO KNOW

dugout—a low shelter that holds the players' bench

full count—when a batter has three balls and two strikes

inning—a unit of play time in which each team takes turns playing offense and defense until three outs are made

perfect game—a game in which a pitcher plays at least nine innings and does not allow a batter to reach first base

shutout—a game in which a pitcher plays a complete game and does not allow the opposing team to score a run

strike zone—the area over home plate from between a batter's chest to the batter's knees

walk-off home run—a home run that gives the home team the lead and the win at the end of a game

wild pitch—a pitch that the catcher is unable to control

windup—the motion a pitcher makes as he is about to throw the ball

GLOSSARY

accuracy (AK-yer-uh-see)—the quality of being exact or free from mistakes

advantage (ad-VAN-tij)—something that helps a player or team achieve success

advice (ad-VAHYS)—suggestions offered to improve someone's actions or performance

concentrate (KAHN-suhn-trayt)—to focus your thoughts and attention on something

confident (KAHN-fi-duhnt)—sure of oneself and abilities

drill (DRIL)—an exercise that is done repeatedly to perfect one's skill or ability

embarrassed (em-BA-ruhsst)—to feel ashamed or self-conscious about one's actions

intimidate (in-TIM-i-dayt)—to overwhelm someone with superior talent or skill so they become timid or fearful

legacy (LEG-uh-see)—qualities or achievements that one is remembered for

recruit (ri-KROOT)—to ask someone to join a company or organization, such as a sports team

reliable (ri-LYE-uh-buhl)—trustworthy or dependable

specialty (SPESH-uhl-tee)—an ability or action in which one shows special skills

stance (STANS)—the position of the body and feet from which an athlete takes action

ABOUT THE AUTHOR

Daniel Mauleón writes comics and books for children and young adults. His professional baseball career started and ended with tee-ball, but he enjoys cheering for the Minnesota Twins. He lives with his wife and two cats in Minnesota.

ABOUT THE ARTISTS

Berenice Muñiz is a graphic designer and illustrator from Monterrey, Mexico. She has done work for publicity agencies, art exhibitions, and even created her own webcomic. These days, Berenice is devoted to illustrating comics as part of the Graphikslava crew.

Francesca Ingrassia is a young Italian colorist and comic book artist based in Palermo, Sicily. She graduated at the "Michelangelo Buonarroti High School" and then moved to Palermo in 2016 to attend a three year school of comics, graduating in 2019. She immediately began to take her first steps in the publishing industry, working mainly as a colorist for If Editions, Heroic Publishing, GFB group, and others.

Giulia Campobello is an Italian comic book and storyboard artist based in Palermo, Sicily. She graduated in modern literature in 2016 and then attended a three-year school of comics and animation in Palermo, graduating in 2019. She mainly works as a storyboard artist and also as a colorist for If Editions, Heroic Publishing, GFB group, and others.

Jaymes Reed has operated the company Digital-CAPS: Comic Book Lettering since 2003. He has done lettering for many publishers, most notably Avatar Press. He's also the only letterer working with Inception Strategies, an Aboriginal-Australian publisher that develops social comics with public service messages for the Australian government. Jaymes is a 2012 and 2013 Shel Dorf Award Nominee.